This book is for you if...

You have a desire to serve God fully
or you are looking for ways
to be a blessing
to your church.

The book will help you
take the right decisions

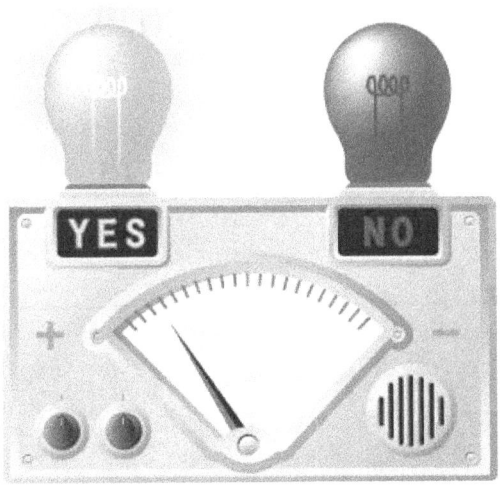

"Now to Him who is able
to do exceedingly
abundantly above
all that we ask or think,
according to the power
that works in us."

Ephesians 3:20.

Called to Serve

By Roselie Emmanuel

Published by
Filament Publishing Ltd
16, Croydon Road,
Waddon, Croydon
Surrey CR0 4PA
United Kingdom
+44 (0)20 8688 2598
www.filamentpublishing.com

© 2015 Roselie Emmanuel

ISBN 978-1-910125-56-4

The right of Roselie Emmanuel to be identified as the author of this work has been asserted by her in accordance with the Designs and Copyright Act 1988.

This book is subjected by international copyright and may not be copied in any way without the prior written permission of the publisher.

Printed by IngramSpark

DEDICATION

I dedicate this book to

To my very special husband
Wil
And our sons
Shane and Seth.

Your patience, prayers and support
made all the difference.

Thank you Pastor Chris Gbenle
for all your support and prayers.

Psalm 113:3.

Thank you Lord, for making
this dream come true.

Your promises
have been
thoroughly tested,
and your servant
loves them.

Psalm 119:140

Contents

Introduction by Pastor Chris Gbenle — 9

Introduction: How to be a good destiny helper — 11

Chapter 1. Keep your promises — 13

Chapter 2. Keep your word — 19

Chapter 3. Sow good seeds at all times — 29

Chapter 4. Benefits of giving — 41

Chapter 5. Pray for your pastor always — 53

Chapter 6. Submission — 65

Chapter 7. The four temperaments — 75

Chapter 8. Soul winning — 79

Chapter 9. Reaching out to others — 85

Chapter 10. Dying to self — 95

Chapter 11. Building healthy relationships — 109

Chapter 12. Prophesy positively over your church — 113

Chapter 13. Pastor's appreciation — 121

Each of you should use
whatever gift you have received
to serve others,
as faithful stewards
of God's grace
in its various forms.

1 Peter 4:10

Introduction
By Pastor Chris Gbenle

Called to Serve is a timely addition to the rich treasure of highly recommended Christian resources available in our time. The author addresses one of the greatest challenges church leaders face - lack of committed workers. The passion and boldness with which the book is written makes it all the more captivating and at the same time challenging.

The chapter on submission is so practical and pointed that rarely will anyone read it without seeing something to work on prayerfully.

The addition of suggested prayer points at the end of each chapter is a testament to the powerful desire of the author to see the body of Christ change more to the image of Christ the head. The prayer points are worth looking at and better still prayed to God.

This is a very well written book, and I recommend it to you. Enjoy it.

Dr. Chris Gbenle
(RCCG Scotland Provincial Pastor)

May the Lord now
show you kindness
and faithfulness,
and I too will show you
the same favor
because you have
done this.

2 Samuel 2:6

Introduction
How to be a good destiny helper

I am really excited and thank God for allowing me the opportunity to write this book.

It has taken me so many years. I am touched by people who have encouraging ministries. I strongly believe that each and every individual has a gift in them which they can use to help further the Kingdom of God.

I have spent a lot of time wondering and praying and asking God how I can be a good role model, leave a positive legacy and make an impact during my time and for future generations.

I have noticed that most of us are interested in what God or the church can do for us and not what we can do for God and the church.

I am hoping and praying that this book will help those who have a desire to serve God fully and those who are looking for ways to be a blessing to their church.

May God bless you mightily as you seek ways to serve Him.

Roselie Emmanuel.

"Lazy people want much
but get little,
but those who work hard
will prosper."

Proverbs 13:4 (NLT).

Chapter 1
Keep your promises

It is very important to keep one's promises and commitments to serving God. I strongly recommend that before you commit to any given task and church you should make sure that you have considered other alternatives.

One should be able to serve God freely and joyfully so it is important to look for a church you understand. Above all you should be happy with the pastor and his doctrine. It is important to find a home church that you can commit to completely. There is no need to be moving from one church to another.

In this day and age there are so many faith ministries—and more springing up every day—so it's no wonder that many unbelievers are confused. It is important to have a church to call home. You can always support other ministries, but everyone needs a place where they are fed spiritually and where their needs can be met. How can you be a blessing to a ministry or pastor if you have not yet found your home? No one will be responsible for you.

If you commit to a ministry and something goes wrong you always get support. You can call for your pastor's support any time and he or she will come happily because they know that you are a committed member of their ministry.

Before committing to a church check everything out, test all the waters to avoid any future regrets. I personally encourage that you pray big time for God's guidance before committing to any church! We need to seek God's guidance so He can place us in the right place where we can be blessed and also be a blessing.

Things to consider before joining or committing to a new ministry:

- Do you believe in the same things doctrine-wise?
- Is it a place where your spiritual needs can be met?
- What is the prayer lifestyle of the church? Does it fit in with your requirements?
- Does it have a prayer department?
- What is their praise and worship team like?
- Do they pray or speak in tongues?
- Is it a place where you and your family can grow?
- Are there any courses or seminars that would be of benefit to you and the community?
- Does the ministry only focus on its members?
- Does the ministry have a heart for the unsaved souls and the community at large?

- Is it a place you'd be proud to invite your family, friends visitors and work colleagues?
- What do you have to lose or gain when you commit?
- Is there a place for you in the ministry? And if so, is it something you can easily fit into?
- Where do you see yourself in future?
- Why do you want to be in this place?
- What are the benefits of you being part of this ministry?
- What can you bring to this ministry?
- What is the support network like?
- Is it a happy place?
- Is it a family-friendly environment?
- Do you feel you are part of the ministry?

I always find it interesting when I hear people complain about certain ministries. If it is not for you, leave it for those who can cope with it!

I remember a certain couple who seemed so excited at being part of my home church when they first started attending. We were arranging a church retreat to Peterhead. I asked the couple if they were joining us and they said they were not ready to commit to anything yet as they were still in the process of praying and checking out the ministry to see if all of their family would fit in. How wise they were!

Laziness brings
on deep sleep,
and the shiftless
go hungry.

Proverbs 19:15

I was so encouraged when six months later the family started serving in church. I knew they had prayed about it. They had considered it together as a couple before getting involved. If you do not pray and think things through before you commit it may be hard to remain faithful when the going gets tough.

It is important for a couple to get involved in the Christian community and church together. Finding a local church where both husband and wife can grow spiritually and socially is very important for every married couple. It is good to attend church together in a place where you both feel comfortable because it will help you serve God and others—and you will make new friends along the way.

Pray and discuss with your spouse before committing to anything in church. Whatever it is make sure it fits well with your family, lifestyle, and work. Once you commit to something make sure you remain faithful. You should not be ashamed or allow anyone to pressure you for commitment before you are certain. If you are not too sure where to go and what to do, you can always tell your pastor that you have not decided yet and are willing to commit only to short-term projects until you have made up your mind.

This is a very good idea: you are able to serve, you avoid slothfulness and inactivity, and you haven't made any promises that you may want to break later on.

"If a house
is divided
against itself,
that house
cannot stand."

(Mark 3:25).

Chapter 2
Keep your word

Once you have committed yourself to something you should remain faithful to it. Giving up will result in you letting down those you have committed to. When volunteering in church, you should perform just as if you're getting paid for the job. Just because you're volunteering does not mean work should be done shabbily. It is good to keep to your word. Before committing to anything, make sure you are fully convinced in your heart about whatever you are going to do. The onus is on you.

When you volunteer to do something do it wholeheartedly and you will be blessed. Failure to perform or doing a shabby job will result in you letting down your team and ruining the morale of those involved.

"But who so looketh into the perfect Law of liberty, and continueth therein, he being not a forgetful hearer, but a doer of the work, this man shall be blessed in his deed."

James 1:25.

"The trustworthy person
will get a rich reward,
but a person who wants
quick riches
will get into trouble."

Proverbs 28:20.

Think before you act

It is better not to offer to help at all than to offer and fail to perform, or, to offer and do a bad job. Think before you act. Put yourself in the shoes of the person or people you are committing to. When you are working as a team, always remember that many hands make light work. It is good to do your part. You also have to remember that sometimes there are situations that cannot be avoided; an emergency for example. If you have to rush to the hospital or go to work your team will understand.

> **"...he honours those who fear the LORD; He who swears to his own hurt and does not change."**
>
> **Psalm 15:4.**

You need to believe in the ministry you decide to join. Believe in your leader or pastor. You need to buy into your pastor's vision. If the pastor is truly a man or a woman after God's heart then all his steps will be ordered by the Lord. This means the vision he is carrying is the vision God has given him.

I think it is very important to do what benefits your pastor most rather than what you feel or think she requires.

Avoid joining a ministry or department thinking you will play it by ear and see how it goes. If you decide to join or stay you must be prepared to defend the integrity of your leader and ministry confidently and without an ounce of doubt. You do not want to be a Judas Iscariot.

While making decisions on whether to stay in a ministry/department or not, ask yourself a lot of questions and try and find answers. Pray and fast if you can for guidance.
Don't stay if you cannot answer your questions or if you aren't satisfied. My advice is for you to leave if you cannot commit to the ministry.

You must be fully convinced in your heart about anything you are involved in. You can never be loyal to a pastor or ministry if you do not trust him. You need to buy into their ministry and desire to be a part of it.

Serve as soon as you can

There may be an area in which you'd like to serve in, but there is no room for you yet. Look for a temporary place to start working in. Make it known to your leader that you are very much interested in joining the choir or ushering department but you will serve in any department until a vacancy arises in that area. This will help you mix with other church members whom you would not have worked with had you got the opportunity to work in your preferred department.

You will learn to appreciate what other departments do and the challenges they face. Be open to serve anywhere. Wherever you are make the best of it. Make an impact in that department even if you know it is not where you are supposed to be. Serve joyfully and willingly. Avoid looking at your job as just another chore: you are making a difference in whatever area you are working in.

Think about the impact you are making. I'm sure if that department was of no use to the church it wouldn't be there! So you are there for a purpose; how to fulfil that purpose depends on you and how far you are willing to go for Christ.

> ## "A faithful man will abound with blessings..."
>
> ### Proverbs 28:20.

"Whatever is true,
whatever is noble,
whatever is right,
whatever is pure,
whatever is lovely,
whatever is admirable—
if anything is excellent
or praiseworthy—
think about such things."

Philippians 4:8.

Everyone has a part to play

We are all employed to do different jobs. For example, hospitals have surgeons, house officers, nurses, phlebotomists, porters, technicians, researchers, cleaners, and kitchen staff. It is the same in the church. We all have to play our own part well. Teamwork makes light work. Desire to be part of the solution to the church rather than being a creator of problems. Get noticed for the right reasons.

If you decide to help in the children's department you cannot say, "I'm only willing to teach and give out snacks but I don't want to help with changing nappies, cleaning and tidying up, or doing the dishes."

Just imagine an usher saying they are willing to greet people but they don't want to show people where to sit!
If you are asked to lend a hand on your day off because a member is sick or running late, you should just go and help.

You promised to be there to serve.

Prayer Points

You will find a list of prayer points at the end of most of the chapters. Please feel free to add your own as these are just suggestions to help you get started.

1. Lord, help me to find a place of worship suitable for me and my family.
2. Pray for wise leaders who inspire respect from those under their command (Romans 13:1).
3. "May Your unfailing love rest upon us, O LORD, even as we put our hope in You." Psalm 33:22.
4. Pray for courage and dependence on God (Psalm 91).
5. Pray for perseverance to endure tough times in the ministry (Isaiah 43:2).
6. Pray for divine protection from the enemy and all his devices (Romans 5:1-5).
7. Pray for confidence and vision to persist. The strength to keep on keeping on.
8. Pray for pastors and departmental heads who are divinely appointed to deliver hope and spiritual strength (Proverbs 4:11).

9. A return to the absolutes of God's Word (Psalm 1:1-3).

10. Integrity—that God's people look and act differently than the world (1 Peter 2:11; 1 Corinthians 12:6).

11. A holy fear of the Lord released in the heart of God's people (Proverbs 9:10).

12. Pray for unity and love among church members (Romans 12:9-13).

13. Pray for the church to find a new zeal and commitment to the mission and purpose of Jesus Christ (Matt 22:37).

14. Pray for diligence.

15. Pray against slothfulness.

"Owe no one anything except to love one another, for he who loves another has fulfilled the law."

1 Corinthians 13 vs 9.

Chapter 3
Sow good seeds at all times

I am passionate about giving and strongly believe that it is one of the best ways you can thank God and bless your church. When I talk about giving I'm not just talking about giving financially. You can give your time and skills, helping to do a number of things to further God's kingdom. You can pray for your pastor and all the other leaders who are working with her. You can intercede for others. You can show your support by attending church programmes and encouraging your pastor with your Hallelujahs and Amen.

If you do not sow seeds how can you expect a harvest? Giving removes focus from self and opens an opportunity for you to reach out to others. I remember hearing a preacher go through the process of drinking some water. When you open the tap the water feeds the tap first before it pours out into the glass. The same thing happens when we bless others. We will be the first partakers of God's reward and blessing, as He answers our prayer to bless, heal and meet our friend's needs. God will bless us as He honours our requests.

So do not ever hesitate or pause to think when it comes to praying for God to bless your pastor, church and family members or friends. You will be the first beneficiary of the blessing. This should not be our main focus though: the greatest thing above all is the pouring out of love.

A gift of substance

Barnabas (which means Son of Encouragement), sold his field and used the proceeds to take care of others. He was a clever and wise man for he was able to recognise the talent that was in Paul and John. Not only did Barnabas recognise the talent that was in others, but he also went a step further to encourage and support them.

Now, how many people see someone starting something good and encourage and support him or her? If it is something that has never been done before people are good at discouraging each other. Just because no one has ever done it or because others have tried and failed does not mean it is impossible! Your words of encouragement to the pastor and other brethren are valuable seeds. When you encourage others, I believe God will also send people to encourage you whenever you are feeling discouraged. I believe Barnabas' giving is a fine example of the way God intended for brethren to live and work together in unity and harmony.

Ephesians 2:10 refers to giving as some kind of super and unique knowledge and skill that God has put within us. Working together, helping and giving to each other are part of God's plan for our lives. At any time I find myself not giving I always feel as if I have moved away from God's plan.

Be genuine

Always be genuine in your giving. The giving must be genuine and one should not be seeking for any reward. Do not be people-pleasers but God lovers and true worshippers. I have seen and heard about 'eye service' within the church: is the pastor watching? Is he looking at me and seeing how well I'm serving? Why should he watch you?

The pastor has got his own problems for which he will answer before God, one fine day. He has his own job to attend to. Give cheerfully because you want to and not because someone else is watching. God is watching and He is the only one who matters.

> "For do I now persuade men, or God?
> Or do I seek to please men?
> For if I still pleased men, I would not be a bondservant of Christ."
>
> **Galatians 1:10.**

"Be careful not to do your 'acts of righteousness' before men, to be seen by them. If you do, you will have no reward from your Father in heaven."

Matthew 6:1.

If you have been waiting or trusting in God for a marriage partner, for healing, the fruit of the womb, financial breakthrough, or academic success, there may be times when you feel led to do something unusual to provoke God and see if He will open the heavens for you in that area. You can provoke God by planting a seed/giving a donation to a ministry or charitable organisation in line with what you are yearning to receive from Him. For example if you are praying to God for a child, you could donate something to an adoption agency, or, if you are hoping for financial breakthrough, you could make a special donation to your church.

What motivates you to give?

Hypocrisy can cost one's life. Remember the story of Ananias and Sapphira? They saw what Barnabas had done by encouraging the brethren. They envied the praises that were given to him by the people. Barnabas had not given because he wanted praise. He was just touched by the passion in the apostles and was moved to do something.

Of their own accord, Ananias and Sapphira decided to sell their land and give the proceeds to the church, but after selling they became greedy and withheld some of the money. They wanted to reap what they had not sown in the form of praises.

Beware: cheating and deceit can rob one of a lot of blessings from God. Watch out for what motivates you to give.

When you give how much do you give? Giving is not about what others have given but a personal thing. You can give a penny but, if it is all you have and it is from the bottom of your heart, heaven will open up for you. Remember: all praises belong to God. When you sow from the heart, He always blesses you in return.

God has given the most priceless gift to mankind and no one can ever match what He bestowed upon us. I know some people have tried to mimic this type of sacrificial giving but it does not carry as much weight as the one our Lord and Saviour Jesus Christ gave. His reason for this wonderful sacrificial gift was to show His love for us. No matter how much you give, you can never out-give God.

What is the reason behind your giving? Is it guilt or shame? Is it pride? Is it because you also have a need that you are hoping God will fulfil? If so what happens when that need has been met? Are you giving to say thank you to God, for the wonderful things He has done for you?

Are you giving because someone has requested your help? Are you giving because you are going to benefit from your generosity? Do you do it for the honour and respect you will receive from others? Is it for your own personal gratification? Is it for God's name to be exalted? Is it for a worthy cause? Is it from love? Why are you giving???
Selah!

No good deed goes unrewarded

Dorcas (Tabitha) was a very kind, caring and giving individual. She had laboured for others and had given herself until she was drained and therefore broke down.

"At Joppa there was a certain disciple called Tabitha which is translated Dorcas. This woman was full of good works and charitable deeds which she did."

Acts 9:36.

We thank God for the wonderful and grateful friends Dorcas blessed when she was fit. God will never forget our acts of love. God will always be there and He remembers all our deeds, both great and small. There is no good deed that will ever go unrewarded.

When people thought Dorcas's life was over, God sent Peter to restore her to health. She received the gift of life because of her good works.

Who knows? What you give today may open many more opportunities in your life. Maybe it is the key to solving all your problems. I believe God wants to restore and bless us with wonderful gifts in the same way that he restored Dorcas. The Lord will truly restore all those who have given in one way or another without any complaint. Sometimes we give in different areas of our lives and end up being drained and spent; but as long as we gave joyfully out of love we should not worry for the Lord will surely restore us. When we give to the things of God it is like saving our money in a savings account.

I also feel that we need to employ wisdom in our giving. Who are we blessing? If the people had not loved Dorcas enough to ask for her life back she would have remained dead.

How is the fulfilment of vision meant to work in practical terms? Here is a powerful statement that reveals the answer:

> ## "A man's gift makes room for him, and brings him before great men."
>
> ## Proverbs 18:16. (NKJV).

The Bible in Proverbs 18:16 clearly tells us that our area of gifting or the talent we have within us will open a door of blessings for us. We should use whatever gifting we have to make an impact in our communities, as we will never know how it might help us when we are in need. Dorcas used the talent she had to bless those around her which resulted in them crying out for her when she had died.

What do you have in your hand which will cause people to cry out to God when you are in trouble or in need? You were designed to be known for something. I think Dorcas did what she knew best and what she loved to do without expecting anything in return apart from maybe the usual payment for services. The people in her community appreciated her services and when she died they wanted her back.

My suggestion is for you to do what you love and to bless the people around you with your talent.

God is totally committed to you and me. He showed this by sending His one and only begotten son, Jesus Christ.

> **"And I will gladly spend and be spent for your souls; though the more abundantly I love you, the less I am loved."**
>
> **2 Corinthians 12: 15.**

Always be willing to give

Your pastor and the church need you even when it is not convenient for you. The Israelites won the battle against the Amalekites just because Aaron and Hur were willing to support their leader. They saw what was happening. Aaron and Hur had gone to the top of the hill to watch the battle with their leader. They were sensitive people, therefore they observed that each time Moses' hands were up the Israelites were winning and whenever he got tired and put his hands down they started losing and the Amalekites started winning. So Aaron and Hur decided to help Moses by holding his arms up until they won the battle. "But Moses' hands became heavy; so they took a stone and put it under him, and he sat on it. And Aaron and Hur supported his hands, one on one side, and the other on the other side; and his hands were steady until the going down of the sun.

So Joshua defeated Amalek and his people with the edge of the sword."

Exodus 17:12-13.

The Israelites were able to defeat the Amalekites because Aaron and Hur observed their pastor in action and noticed what was happening. When they noticed their leader getting tired they made him comfortable and helped to support his arms.

Moses was blessed to have such good, faithful and devoted followers.

This also applies to you and me. We should keep a careful eye on our pastor. We should be aware of when she is in need of our support and jump in to help her. By lifting up our pastor's hands through prayer and doing the work of the ministry diligently we can do great exploits in our church and community. Spirits fighting against the body of Christ will be defeated. Many will give their lives to Christ.

Don't just be there when things are going smoothly. Be there when times are tough because that is when your pastor needs you most. Aaron and Hur were there with Moses "...until the going down of the sun." They were there when Moses needed them most. They did not give up. Yes, the day was long. Yes, the going was tough. But they persevered together with their leader until the battle was won.

Support your pastor

What concerns does your leader have that require your immediate attention and action? What is happening in your community that is causing your pastor to go up on the hill to war? Are you going to follow him and help? Your pastor needs you and he cannot win any battles without your support.
He needs your prayers, he needs your time, and he needs your financial and physical support too. In order to win the battle, Moses needed Aaron and Hur and vice versa. The story of how the children of Israel defeated Amalek is enough evidence to me that togetherness is the way forward for any ministry or any group of people who want to achieve something.

Paul gladly offered himself for the work of the Lord. It was not easy for him but he persevered because he was committed. He was a supporter of God's work in a mighty big way. He was a complete giver. I hope and pray that the good Lord will grant us the wonderful grace of being committed to His work and therefore continuing to give and give to His worthwhile cause.

Prayer Points

1. Lord I am available and willing.

2. If you can use anything Lord, use me.

3. May I be an Aaron or Hur to my pastor.

4. May I be in the right place at the right time.

5. May I be part of the answer.

6. May I buy into the vision you have given my pastor.

Chapter 4
Benefits of giving

Giving is one way of opening your channel of blessings from God and from those around you. Learn to look at giving as a form of sowing. I liken giving to sowing because when you sow you reap. You always get much more or much better than what you give. Your giving can transform a life or bring hope to a hopeless situation.

1. When you give constantly, you will continue to reap joyfully and bountifully.

You will continue to flourish and reap spiritually and financially too. If we desire a continual flow of both spiritual and financial blessings we need to continue planting whenever we get the chance.

> **"Give, and it will be given to you: good measure, pressed down, shaken together, and running over will be put into your bosom. For with the same measure that you use, it will be measured back to you."**
> **Luke 6:38 (NKJV).**

"Now may He who supplies
seed to the sower,
and bread for food,
supply and multiply the seed
you have sown and increase
the fruits of your righteousness,"

2 Corinthians 9:8-10 (NKJV).

Whether you sow happily or in tears, God will multiply it.
2 Corinthians 9:8 says;

"⁸ And God is able to make all grace abound toward you, that you, always having all sufficiency in all things, may have an abundance for every good work."

Psalms 112:9 King James Version (KJV)

"⁹ He has dispersed abroad,
He has given to the poor;
His righteousness endures forever;
horn shall be exalted with honour."

2. God blesses us so we can be a blessing to others.

The more we prosper the more we are able to give and help others. When we bless others that means they also have an opportunity to grow and when they grow they can become blessings to others as well.

Your giving will give birth to more givers. This means that there will be many lenders in the land and the burden will not be solely on you. When we give to the church we are actually sowing to the community because that money or time we have invested can be spent feeding the poor, winning more souls and providing a place for worship. Once more souls are added to the church it means less crime because you will have created a God-fearing community.

The church bills need to be paid. Transport is required to mobilise people and every little you give goes a long way. When you bless people you are actually teaching them how to be a blessing to others. Your generous giving will change lives in your community.

3.   It is good to encourage your pastor by giving.

It blesses him and the church as a whole. The work of the ministry can be slow. So many things can be going on in a pastor's life. Sometimes the going may be tough but because they know they are there for your benefit they have to remain positive, keep smiling, keep moving, keep teaching and keep encouraging you. When he is facing challenges, whether they are financial or family issues, your pastor and his wife will really appreciate your support and well wishes.

This reminds me of a joke I once heard. Someone was passing by a house early one Sunday morning and he overheard a conversation between a mother and her son.

The son was refusing to go to church saying he was very tired and that he had been going to church every Sunday for the past 10 years. The son complained that the people were mean, they did not like him, they did not appreciate him and he was tired of going to a place that brought him down all the time.

The passerby felt so sorry for the son—until he heard the mother say in a strong stern voice: "You are the pastor! You have to go to church. What is your congregation going to say?"

That congregation must have been something else I think! May we create a beautiful place of worship for ourselves and our pastor. May we all enjoy being in the house of the Lord just like King David did.

Psalms 122:1

> **"I was glad when they said unto me,
> Let us go into the house of the LORD."**

4.   Experience the intervention of God in our lives.

One of the most exciting reasons to give is that we can experience the intervention of God in our lives in a very real and mind-blowing way.

Deuteronomy 6:16 says we should not put God to the test. However, there is one exception to this and we find it in Malachi 3:10 where the Lord himself dares his people to test his faithfulness by tithing faithfully and seeing if he will not shower them with blessings.

> **"You shall not tempt the LORD your God as you tempted Him in Massah."**
>
> **Deuteronomy 6:16.**

And:

> **"Bring all the tithes into the storehouse,**
> **That there may be food in My house,**
> **And try Me now in this,"**
> **Says the LORD of hosts,**
> **"If I will not open for you**
> **the windows of heaven**
> **And pour out for you such blessing**
> **That there will not be room**
> **enough to receive it."**
>
> **Malachi 3:10.**

5.   Whatever we do for others, so we do unto the Lord.

Another major reason to give is because we are told in the Bible that as we give to the work of the Kingdom and in particular the people of God, God will count it as a personal favour such that whatever we do for his children, we do it also unto the Lord.

Let's say you're a parent. Your children get stranded somewhere on their way home from school and someone goes out of their way to help them. Wouldn't you thank them sincerely for it? How much more do you think our heavenly Father is able to do for you?

We can't give our money to God personally, but when we give our money in His name to those around us in order to draw them into the Kingdom of God, it would be considered as good as giving to God himself.

> "He who receives you receives Me, and he who receives Me receives Him who sent Me."
> Matthew 10:40.

> "And the King will answer and say to them,
> 'Assuredly, I say to you,
> inasmuch as you did it
> to one of the least of these
> My brethren, you did it to Me'."
>
> Matthew 25:40.

> "For God is not unjust to forget your work and labour of love which you have shown toward His name, in that you have ministered to the saints, and do minister."
> Hebrews 6:10.

> "But do not forget to do good and to share, for with such sacrifices God is well pleased."
> Hebrews 16:13.

> "He who has pity on the poor
> lends to the LORD,
> And He will pay back what he has given."
> **Proverbs 19:17.**

6.   Life is better for the giving Christian.

Jesus confirms that life will be much, much better for the giving Christian rather than for the non-giving Christian.

> "I have shown you in every way, by labouring like this, that you must support the weak.
> And remember the words of the Lord Jesus, that He said,
> 'It is more blessed to give than to receive'."
>
> **Acts 20:35.**

> "Give, and it will be given to you: good measure, pressed down, shaken together, and running over will be put into your bosom. For with the same measure that you use, it will be measured back to you."
>
> Luke 6:38.

7.   A rich harvest.

God will take a seed from you and with that seed He will create a harvest for you.

8.   Give and the Lord gives too.

When you get involved and invest in your church's dream, the Lord will get involved and will also invest in your affairs in a mighty way. You will be like them that dream.

Prayer Points

1. Lord, help me to be on time.
2. Lord, help me to be spiritually sensitive.
3. Lord, help me to be there for my pastor when he needs my support.
4. Lord, help me do and give the best I can at all times.
5. Lord, allow me the grace to listen to you and to hear from you constantly.
6. Show me where I should serve.
7. May I be a good example to the younger generation.
8. Lord, I know I do not qualify to serve in your house. Clean me, build me up, strengthen me and qualify me.
9. Lord, help me not to draw attention to myself.

Apostle Paul requested prayers:

"Finally, brethren, pray for us,
that the word of the Lord may
run swiftly and be glorified,
just as it is with you,
and that we may be delivered
from unreasonable and wicked men;
for not all have faith."

2 Thessalonians 3:1-2.

"And He Himself gave some to be apostles, some prophets, some evangelists, and some pastors and teachers, for the equipping of the saints for the work of ministry, for the edifying of the body of Christ, till we all come to the unity of the faith and of the knowledge of the Son of God, to a perfect man, to the measure of the stature of the fullness of Christ..."

Ephesians 4:11-16 (NKJV).

Chapter 5
Pray for your pastor always

Pastors are human too!

Serving as a pastor is a remarkable and awesome blessing and privilege, but sometimes pastors can be the most misunderstood people in the church. Often their hours are long, the pay minimal, the criticism considerable and constant. Despite the joys of serving God, feelings of disappointment and discouragement can plague the best of them.

Our pastors are very human. They are not perfect and they make mistakes just like you and I. They also need time, love, care and our support. We tend to over-criticise the mistakes they make and even their children's behaviour.

Praying for your pastor will cause the anointing in your church to increase and you will receive more blessings. Failure to pray can rob or deny you of your spiritual blessings.

A pastor is one of Christ's five office gifts to the church:

A gift from God

Pastoring is a gift from God. A pastor is a GIFT that God gives to a church. The term pastor comes from 'shepherd', one who guides and cares for a flock.

They are just as susceptible to falling and failing as you and I. They are our leaders and we need to pray for them. If you are looking for someone to pray for please do not forget to pray for your pastor. He needs all the prayers and support you can give. Pray, pray, pray for your pastor—you know how much opposition you face yourself... from the world, the flesh, and the devil... and be assured, your pastor has much more to deal with than you do. Pray for him every day, and ask God to shower your pastor with an abundance of love, hope, joy, faith, peace, power, wisdom, holiness and courage.

Pray for your spiritual leader's maturity and growth in the faith. The German writer, Johann Wolfgang von Goethe wrote: "If you treat a person as he is, he will stay as he is; but if you treat him as if he were what he ought to be, he will become what he ought to be and could be."

Give your pastor proper and genuine respect:

> "And we urge you, brethren, to recognize those who labour among you, and are over you in the Lord and admonish you, and to esteem them very highly in love for their work's sake..."
> 1 Thessalonians 5:12-13.

Respect your pastor

Treat him with the same or even more respect than you would anyone else in authority. Sometimes people tend to think of their pastor as an employee instead of their spiritual leader. Our pastor needs our respect. He is God's appointed man, to help and guide you and your family's souls.

Express your respect for her authority by addressing her as 'pastor' rather than by her first name, especially while on church premises. In the outside world, give her all due respect and call her by her title unless she gives you permission to address her by her first name.

> "Let the elders who rule well be counted worthy of double honour, especially those who labour in the word and doctrine."
> 1 Timothy 5:17.

I really want to thank God for what he is doing in my life. In the past I used to talk about the wrongs and the shortcomings of my pastors. I later realised that I was being used by the enemy to cause misunderstandings in our church. Yes there have been quite a number of things that were not right but the Holy Spirit taught me to take everything to God in prayer. Rather than picking up the phone and talking to a friend about the bad things I heard or I experienced, I decided to pray about it and ask God to perfect all that concerned my leader. I have never felt better.

Gossiping about your pastor is a very bad move. One day you will answer for it before God. My advice is to pray for your pastor consistently. The more you pray for your pastor the less you see his shortcomings. The best thing to do for yourself is to isolate yourself from people or friends who enjoy talking about the pastor and his family behind his back. I did and the benefits and peace of mind I have now are amazing.

"Do not touch My anointed ones, and do My prophets no harm." Psalm 105:15.

Avoid those who cause division

Stay away from the negative people who are always complaining. If they can gossip to you about the pastor what is going to stop them gossiping about you?

> "Now I urge you, brethren, note those who cause divisions and offences, contrary to the doctrine which you learned, and avoid them."
> **Romans 16:17.**

> "A perverse man sows strife, and a whisperer separates the best of friends."
> **Proverbs 16:28.**

The above scripture says 'note' them which means know them and, once you know them, avoid them. You can still greet and talk to them but avoid spending unnecessary time with them. Remember to pray for them. Remember they need deliverance. In Proverbs 6, we are clearly informed of the seven things the Lord hates. In verse 19 we learn that He hates:
"One who sows discord among brethren."

If you do not want to pray for your pastor, would you join with me to pray for mine?

Pray the word of God

Pray the word of God and God's will over your pastor. When you use the word of God in praying for your pastor you never pray amiss.

a)	Pray for blessings. For your pastor and his family's needs to be met. Spiritual, financial, emotional and physical.
Use 2 Corinthians 9:8:

"And God is able to make all grace (every favour and earthly blessing) come to you in abundance, so that you may always and under all circumstances and whatever the need be self-sufficient [possessing enough to require no aid or support and furnished in abundance for every good work and charitable donation]."

And:

"Now it shall come to pass, if you diligently obey the voice of the LORD your God, to observe carefully all His commandments which I command you today, that the LORD your God will set you high above all nations of the earth. 2 And all these blessings shall come upon you and overtake you, because you obey the voice of the LORD your God:

3 'Blessed shall you be in the city, and blessed shall you be in the country.'4 'Blessed shall be the fruit of your body, the produce of your ground and the increase of your herds, the increase of your cattle and the offspring of your flocks.'5 'Blessed shall be your basket and your kneading bowl. '6 'Blessed shall you be when

you come in, and blessed shall you be when you go out.'7 "The LORD will cause your enemies who rise against you to be defeated before your face; they shall come out against you one way and flee before you seven ways.8 "The LORD will command the blessing on you in your storehouses and in all to which you set your hand, and He will bless you in the land which the LORD your God is giving you."

Deuteronomy 28:1-8.

b) Pray for insight and revelation.

Use Ephesians 1:16-19: "do not cease to give thanks for you, making mention of you in my prayers:17 that the God of our Lord Jesus Christ, the Father of glory, may give to you the spirit of wisdom and revelation in the knowledge of Him,18 the eyes of your understanding being enlightened; that you may know what is the hope of His calling, what are the riches of the glory of His inheritance in the saints,19 and what is the exceeding greatness of His power toward us who believe, according to the working of His mighty power."

c) Pray for the Holy Spirit to guide your pastor.

Ask God to bless your pastor with wisdom. Pray for the Holy Spirit to overshadow her, so your pastor is guided to make the right decisions and work with members of her church and the community at large in the right way.

Pray for the Spirit of Truth to come and guide her in all things:

"But when He, the Spirit of Truth (the Truth-giving Spirit) comes, He will guide you into all the Truth (the whole, full Truth). For He will not speak His own message [on His own authority]; but He will tell whatever He hears [from the Father; He will give the message that has been given to Him], and He will announce and declare to you the things that are to come [that will happen in the future]."

John 16: 13.

"Guide me in Your truth and faithfulness and teach me, for You are the God of my salvation; for You [You only and altogether] do I wait [expectantly] all the day long."
Psalm 25: 5.

"Teach me Your way, O Lord, and lead me in a plain and even path because of my enemies [those who lie in wait for me]."
Psalm 27: 11.

"And the Lord shall guide you continually and satisfy you in drought and in dry places and make strong your bones. And you shall be like a watered garden and like a spring of water whose waters fail not."
Isaiah 58: 11.

d)   Pray for protection (for your pastor and their loved ones). "No evil shall befall you, nor shall any plague come near your dwelling;11 For He shall give His angels charge over you, to keep you in all your ways."
Psalm 91:10-11.

"No weapon formed against you shall prosper, and every tongue which rises against you in judgment you shall condemn. This is the heritage of the servants of the LORD, and their righteousness is from Me," says the LORD."

Isaiah 55:17.

e)   Pray for more insight and revelations for your pastor: Use Ephesians 1:17:

"...that the God of our Lord Jesus Christ, the Father of glory, may give to you the spirit of wisdom and revelation in the knowledge of Him..."

And:

"They were amazed at His teaching; He was teaching them as one having authority, and not as the scribes."
Mark 1:22.

f) Pray for help in teaching the word of God and for anointing to rest upon your pastor:

Use Ephesians 6:19:
"...and for me, that utterance may be given to me, that I may open my mouth boldly to make known the mystery of the gospel..."

And:

"The Spirit of the LORD is upon Me, Because He has anointed Me to preach the gospel to the poor; He has sent Me to heal the broken hearted, To proclaim liberty to the captives And recovery of sight to the blind, To set at liberty those who are oppressed...
Luke 4:18.

Prayer Points

Please insert your pastor or leader's name in the verses below as you pray for their love for God and the church and ministry to abound, and for more insight and knowledge of the Lord.

1. Pray for his protection.
2. Pray for guidance from the Holy Spirit.
3. Pray for blessings, spiritual and material.
4. Pray for revelation.
5. Pray for faithfulness: pray that she will be faithful in all that she does, faithful to her commitments, her staff, her spouse and family, but above all pray that she will always be faithful to God and in what God would have her do to accomplish the purpose for her life.
6. Pray for divine rest and good health.
7. Pray for wisdom and divine provision.
8. "Then God said to him:

"Because you have asked this thing,
and have not asked long life for yourself,
nor have asked riches for yourself,
nor have asked the life of your enemies,
but have asked for yourself understanding
to discern justice,
behold, I have done according to your words;
see, I have given you a wise
and understanding heart,
so that there has not been
anyone like you before you, nor shall any
like you arise after you.

And I have also given you what you
have not asked: both riches and honour,
so that there shall not be anyone like you
among the kings all your days."

1 Kings 3:11-13.

Chapter 6
Submission

Follow your pastor as he follows Christ

We are also instructed to follow and imitate those spiritual leaders as they follow Christ. Follow the man of God who is following Jesus Christ as set forth in the Word of God.

"Remember those who rule over you, who have spoken the word of God to you, whose faith follow, considering the outcome of their conduct."

Hebrews 13:7.

Remember what I said earlier on; it is our job to support our pastor's vision. Failure to grasp or accept or support his vision will mean that we are not walking in agreement. It is your pastor's vision that carries more weight in your church so never fool yourself. If you have your own vision that you want to follow my advice to you is to go and start your own ministry and attract like-minded people to support you.

The Bible places special emphasis on submission to spiritual authorities. The writer of Hebrews says:

"Obey those who rule over you,
and be submissive,
for they watch out for your souls,
as those who must give account.
Let them do so with joy
and not with grief,
for that would be
unprofitable for you."

Hebrews 13:17.

Never promote your own vision in another's ministry. You cannot run your ministry from somebody else's church.

If you're not happy with the way your leader is doing things move to another ministry. If you continue to stay under a leadership you are not happy with it will result in bad feeling and rebellion. You will not serve God wholeheartedly.

When you submit you are yielding yourself to the authority or will of your pastor or leader. If your pastor asks you to do something, just follow his instructions. There will be times when you won't agree with the decision but still you have to obey because you trust and believe in the God he serves.

Submission is when you go ahead and do as requested despite the fact that you don't agree with what you have been asked to do. (Maybe you believe you have a better way of doing the same thing). Submission is having an uneducated or poor leader and still respecting and honouring them.

Submit fully

A good attitude is always a good thing! I am one of those people who struggle to do something if I am not happy about it. Sometimes I am forced to do things just because there is no one else to do it. I do not like to do anything grudgingly.

I always desire to do things happily and with a smile. If I can find someone who can do whatever I am not happy to do, I am always glad to hand over the baton and support them joyfully. In recent years the Holy Spirit has been talking to me seriously about it. I felt that I have not been fully submissive as I have always looked for people to do what I do not like doing.

I am praying earnestly that God will continue to help me to submit fully to authority so that on that day I will not be found wanting. I am a work in progress and I thank God for the work He is doing in me. In the past I struggled doing certain things. Why? Because I was doing them all by myself and not letting God take control.

There are many ways of killing a cat; but if you are asked to do something, do it according to instruction. One thing I am pretty sure of is if your pastor or leader is a God-fearing person, they will never ask you to do something that is against the will and word of God. God will never ask His children to be involved in sinful acts or any abusive behaviour.

As long as your leader is under the direction and is in full submission to God's authority there is nothing to worry about. This is the reason why you need to spend time praying before you commit to a church. If you have a lot of unanswered questions, do not commit yourself. It is not worth it. Be very sure.

Accommodate others

Sometimes we have to work with people with different personality types than ours. I am a very emotional person and often struggle to work with people of different temperaments than mine. The issue of submission and obedience has really made me bend over in order to accommodate and work with people whom I would normally avoid because we will never agree on anything. In the past I struggled with working as part of a group because I was so used to doing things on my own. Being part of something requires maturity and it is a very good and safe way to grow because you have other people to share ideas with and who will support you.

Though I prefer one to one meetings, I'm getting much better with working as a member of a team. When you work as a team you can accomplish much.

I remember a few years ago when my pastor told me that I was too sensitive and needed to grow a thicker skin. It was very painful because it was true and I realised I needed to do something about it. For weeks and months afterwards, I found myself singing:

> "One day at a time sweet Jesus
> That's all I'm askin' of you
> Just give me the strength
> To do every day what I have to do
> Yesterday's gone sweet Jesus
> And tomorrow may never be mine
> Lord, help me today, show me the way
> One day at a time."

I really thank God for my pastor who gently pushed me into doing group things. It is only when I started that I began to enjoy working as part of a team. It was not as dull and gloomy as I expected. Teamwork has increased my self esteem. I now find it more rewarding and more important than working as a lone ranger.

Teamwork renders an increase in performance and productivity. In a group you have people with different skills, experience and interests. You also get an opportunity or platform to sharpen your skills. Your listening and speaking skills are developed. You learn more about leadership, how to motivate others, patience, politeness, and self discipline. You get to know yourself more by identifying your own strengths and weaknesses.

The four personality types

There are four temperaments, which are sanguine (pleasure-seeking and sociable), choleric (ambitious and leader-like), melancholic (introverted and thoughtful), and phlegmatic (relaxed and quiet). Please note that it is possible for an individual to have two or three personality types but there will be one that will stand out and be obvious to everyone.

I am a 90% melancholic and have 10% sanguine tendencies—very romantic, compassionate and sensitive. I happen to be married to a phlegmatic who hardly ever shows any emotion at all. He is Mister Cool, Calm and Collected. He is never in a hurry and I am the one who worries about every little detail. I need to plan. I like to make things happen. I thank God because despite our different personality types we still get on like a house on fire! It goes to show that it's possible to work with people who have different personalities than ours - something that I thought was impossible. Anything is possible and for it to be possible you need to put your trust in it.

One thing I have come to realise and accept is if I can be happily married to a man for 20 years who has a completely opposite personality to mine what can stop me from working with another person for a few hours?

Balance is crucial and one has to look at the bigger picture. It is about God not me. I need to focus on the positives and the same goes for you. An extreme mind renewal and change of focus is required.

> **"Finally, brethren,
> whatever things are true,
> whatever things are noble,
> whatever things are just,
> whatever things are pure,
> whatever things are lovely,
> whatever things are of good report,
> if there is any virtue
> and if there is anything praiseworthy -
> meditate on these things."**
>
> **Philippians 4:8.**

I really thank God for Joyce Meyer's books Living Beyond Your Feelings: Controlling Emotions So They Don't Control You and Managing Your Emotions: Instead of Your Emotions Managing You. I have been blessed tremendously by these awesome books.

I am praying that I will be able to put into practice what I have learnt. I have a very strong personality and working with people with different temperaments than mine can be challenging, but since reading the above books I have been working so hard on building up my relationships with people of different temperaments. I used to avoid certain people, but now I find I don't mind talking to them. I am making an extra effort to remove the focus from me and my little space and to take a look at the bigger picture.

> A happy heart makes
> the face cheerful,
> but heartache
> crushes the spirit.
>
> Proverbs 15:13

Prayer Points

1. Help me Lord, to die to self.
2. Lord, increase so I decrease.
3. Give me a heart and spirit that is willing to be corrected.
4. Grant me a teachable and joyful spirit.
5. Let me not insist on my ways when it is hard to submit.
6. Make me a good team player.
7. Grant me the right attitude.
8. When corrected, help me to respond in humility.
9. Help me to forgive and move on peacefully when offences come.
10. Show me the rewards of submission.
11. Grant me the grace to submit not only physically but also spiritually, emotionally and wholeheartedly.
12. Oh Lord! Help me to pass your submission test.
13. Grant me the grace to serve and submit with a smile even in my darkest hour.

Chapter 7
The Four Temperaments

From Joyce Meyer's Managing Your Emotions: Instead of Your Emotions Managing You, I learned that there are four basic personality types. We all are wired differently and your understanding of this will make it easier for you to understand, communicate and work with anyone.

The Sanguine

This is the very sensitive, romantic and compassionate type. Impulsive and pleasure-seeking; sanguine people are sociable and charismatic. They tend to enjoy social gatherings, making new friends and are likely to be boisterous.

They are usually late for meetings, struggle with following tasks to the end and can be forgetful. They are confident and very chatty people. They are usually quite creative and often daydream. However, some alone time is crucial for those of this temperament.

The Choleric

They like to be in charge or dominate everything. They are ambitious go-getters. They are not lukewarm and quickly swing from one extreme to another. They tend to be either highly organised or highly disorganised. They have a lot of aggression, energy, and passion, and often if not always try to force it on others.

Many great political and charismatic figures were choleric. As well as being assertive and natural leaders, they are prone to mood swings that can often result in deep and sudden depression.

The Phlegmatic

The phlegmatic temperament is relaxed and quiet, ranging from warmly attentive to lazily sluggish. Phlegmatics are normally kind, tend to be content with themselves and usually show little or no emotion at all. They are accepting and affectionate. They may be receptive and shy and often prefer stability to uncertainty and change.

They are consistent, relaxed, calm, rational, curious, and observant; qualities that make them good administrators. They can also be passive-aggressive.

The Melancholic

The melancholic temperament is thoughtful and introverted. They are very deep thinkers, perfectionists and very good organisers. They worry about the slightest detail and are the ones who have the most problem with depression. Melancholics can be highly creative in activities such as art and poetry. They can easily become overly preoccupied with the bad things happening to people and in the world. They are very independent and self-reliant. One negative part of being a melancholic is that they can get so engrossed in whatever they are doing that they forget to think of others. Let's just say that they can be selfish!

Search much deeper within

I felt I needed to go over the four personality types so you could understand where I am coming from. If you think you will not be able to work with someone you really need to search deeper because the other person might not be the problem. Maybe the problem lies within you.

Do you struggle with pride or an inferiority complex? You have to change your attitude. Even if your leader or pastor is harsh and abrupt, less educated, or younger, he is still your leader. Submit and serve joyfully.

When you submit it makes the work of the ministry easier for you, your leader and the church. Don't worry about how things are done: as long as your leader is submissive to God all will be well.

"Go ye therefore, and teach all nations,
baptizing them in the name of the Father,
and of the Son, and of the Holy Ghost:

Teaching them to observe all things
whatsoever I have commanded you:
and, lo, I am with you always,
even unto the end of the world."

Matthew 28:19-20.

Chapter 8
Soul winning

Invite your friends, family, neighbours and workmates to church. Start with the people you already talk to and then extend the invitation to strangers. Inviting people to church is a great way to win souls. Soul winning is not only about you leading someone to Christ. It is also about leading someone to a place where they can give their life to Christ. That first step of taking someone to a place of worship is the most important one.

> "He first found his own brother Simon,
> and said to him,
> "We have found the Messiah"
> (which is translated, the Christ).
> And he brought him to Jesus.
> Now when Jesus looked at him,
> He said, "You are Simon the son of Jonah.
> You shall be called Cephas"
> (which is translated, A Stone)."
>
> John 1:41-42.

An awesome way of inviting people to church is during special occasions; for example thanksgiving, baptism, picnics, music concerts, baby dedications, Easter and Christmas. Sometimes you have to give or do something for someone before they will listen to you. I remember one particular time when I met a hairdresser at an exhibition. We got on really well.

A few weeks later I decided to pay her a visit at her salon; she was so excited to see me and she surrendered her life to Christ. I did not have to push things. She only asked me why I was so happy and always smiling and I started explaining to her about the love of God. It was amazing. When I went to visit her I was not expecting her to give her life on that day but it happened. Glory to God!

Pray for your church. It is very difficult to invite people to a church that is full of scandal. Pray for your leaders and the church members. Ask God to help all your leaders and church members to exhibit the love and warmth of Christ in them.

Things like meekness, gentleness and cleanliness are very important. You cannot shout at your husband or wife, the taxi driver, your house cleaner, or workmate and then expect them to turn up for church when you invite them. We need to exhibit the nature of Christ in our lives.

There is no one who is too much of a sinner that God cannot save. It is not up to you to decide that I cannot bring a certain class of people to church or I cannot talk to a certain person. I thank God for not withholding His Son from dying for me. I am not better than anyone. It is Christ in me who makes all the difference and my prayer is that you also will be challenged to win souls for Christ.

Use your personal testimony

People love to hear stories. Repackage your testimony well. How can you do that? Ask God to give you guidance and wisdom in preparing your testimony so you can use it to bring many to him. Be sure your experiences are scriptural before you share them with others. Interpret your experiences by the Word of God and not vice versa. Always remember that the Bible is our authority. Include relevant, thought-provoking facts and experiences. Give it in such a way that others will be able to empathise with you.

A few helpful tips on using your testimony for soul winning:

- Use everyday words that a non-Christian would understand.
- Smile.

Things to avoid:

- Avoid making the person feel bad or guilty.
- Use everyday words that a non-Christian would understand.
- Avoid preaching at them.
- Avoid going on and on and on...
- Avoid mentioning church denominations, especially in a derogatory manner.
- Avoid giving the person the impression that being a Christian is a bed of roses.

Prayer Points

1. Lord, make me a good ambassador for you.
2. Grant me the boldness to speak to people about you.
3. When I go out to evangelise may it be all about you.
4. Bless me with a testimony, so I can go about proclaiming your love and faithfulness in my life.
5. May my testimony tell more about you and not me.
6. Make my church a scandal-free one.
7. Make my church a church I will be proud to invite friends, relatives and neighbours to.

Even as I try to please
everyone in every way.
For I am not seeking my own good
but the good of many,
so that they may be saved.

1 Corinthians 10:33

Chapter 9
Reaching out to others

Most of us live in our own little world concerned only with ourselves and our families. As long as we are alright we do not spend much time thinking of others and their needs. Reaching out can be something we take for granted especially if we do not have any people close to us who are in need. Most people prefer to help people who somebody else is already helping.

God has blessed us human beings with a special gift, and that is our ability to reach out to those around us. When I talk about reaching out it doesn't necessarily mean extending a hand or some other form of physical contact. It also means reaching out with our hearts, minds, souls, and especially our gifts. It seems strange how we live in a technologically advanced world of instant communication and billions of people, but still many of us remain lonely.

Help them to accept your help

You need to reach out to those around you. It's not always easy. You may need to overcome your own hopelessness, loneliness, hurt, pain, fear, regrets and indecision.

There are many people out there who are beaten down by circumstances, physically or mentally ill, or living in fear; and they are incapable of reaching out without a little help from others. Could you be the one to reach out to that person?

I am going to share a personal story with you. I have been unwell since 2003. I struggled for a couple of years without knowing what was wrong. At that time I was the general secretary of the church's women's group. But I was really struggling. I had to go to the hospital for so many tests and treatments and a few days after I had gone for a head scan and some other tests I felt that I needed to step down from my role within the women's group. I attended the next women's committee meeting and explained my problems to them.

Then I announced my intention to step down due to ill health. My leader was not happy with my move and I couldn't understand why she was so unsympathetic about my health. She did not hide her disappointment and she just walked out soon after the meeting.

I felt unloved. I felt no one cared. I was very upset and felt let down by my leader but the truth was that I was the cause of my pain. I had behaved selfishly and immaturely. I was inconsiderate towards my leader. I made it all about me and forgot to consider the effects of my decision on other people.

I had disrespected my leader by resigning from my post in front of the other committee members. I should have gone to her to explain what was going on with me healthwise and notify her of my intention to step down prior to the meeting. There had not been any form of communication between me and my leader about my health. How was she supposed to know what was going on with me if I had not told her?

Take responsibility for your own actions

Just look at how we are so quick to judge and blame others for the pain we are going through due to our own miscalculations. Then, I felt and thought my leader did not like me but now I know better. Things could have been handled a lot better had I behaved with maturity and wisdom. Thank God for maturity and soberness because now I understand more about the power of relationships.

We need to look at our own actions before we assume things and make unjust judgements against our pastor, leader or fellow brethren. I should have spoken to my leader and she should have been the one to announce my intention to step down to the rest of the committee; but I just did my own thing. I want to thank God for opening my eyes, allowing me to see the mistakes I made and giving me a chance to rectify them.

How can my leader reach out to me if I fail to communicate with her? Too often we feel let down by others but fail to realise that we are the reason for others' failure to reach out to us. I never communicated what I was going through and yet I expected my leader to reach out to me. Assumptions can be very costly to relationships!

I knew a lot of people but—due to my failure to communicate—I became lonely. I failed to reach out for help. Sometimes we need to reach out for help rather than blaming people for not reaching out to us. If someone is starving and I have food, I will stretch out my hand to pass on the food to the needy person. The person in need has to reach out to accept the gift of food. If they do not extend their hand to take it I could mistakenly assume they do not want it.

Rather than walking away, I could go that extra mile and ask why they have rejected my gift. The reason could be that someone has already given them something, or they cannot eat the type of food I am offering, or they are in so much pain they cannot stretch out their hand to accept my food; in which case I would then offer to feed them. Yet I could have simply walked angrily away.

We need to learn to reach out with an open and loving heart while at the same time remembering and understanding that sometimes our offer could be rejected. We need to ask God for the grace to move on and reach out to the next person.

Do not be discouraged. Jesus never stopped loving us during our time of ignorance.

People in need

Lonely people and people in pain can be found in every community. What about that elderly couple whose children live abroad, the widow and her three children, the person who has been made redundant, those who are mentally or physically ill? I just want to encourage you to reach out to people in need.

Reach out to the homeless, the orphans, the sick, the widows and the elderly. In winter if your neighbour needs a hand pushing the car; help them. If you see them struggling to clear the snow from their driveway, help if you are able. You need to be available not only to the body of Christ but also to the non-believer so when you invite them to a church meeting or activity they will be willing to support you. They might not be interested in going to church but they will honour your invitation and you never know whether they will become the next house fellowship leader. Are you ready to go the whole distance for Christ?

When people are grieving or hurting, they are open to anyone who reaches out to them. Normally they will join the group that attended to them first. If you want to be of help to the body of Christ, support your pastor by reaching out "...with the love of God to a world that is hurting and insecure..." (Fountain of Love, Aberdeen, Mission Statement).

We really need to wise up and be ready when people need us. Failure to reach out will result in others getting there before us. If there is no community outreach program in your church why don't you start one? If you give someone what they cannot get anywhere else they will keep coming back. What is in your hand? Invite a friend out for a coffee, lunch, a hike. Make it an activity that allows you to talk a bit and catch up. Create time. Some wise person once told me that: "Whatever you are interested in, you will always create time to do it."

Remember to seek your leader or pastor's permission before starting any projects. Spiritual covering and support is very important. Remember you are not doing your pastor a favour: you are really doing yourself a favour. You will grow spiritually; there is no doubt about that.

Look out for your community's needs

I have noticed that different communities are faced with different problems. Look out for your community's needs. Do you have any problems with alcoholism, drug addiction, prostitution, teen pregnancies, abortions, suicides, certain illnesses and homelessness in your area?

What can you do? You could send a note, a card, fruit or flowers to someone you know is not feeling well. Check up on someone you have not seen for a while. Pray for them. Pray with them. Get friendly within reason. Call someone, send them a text. Offer a helping hand for free, e.g. do the dishes, mow their lawn, do some shopping for them. Can you offer a lift to someone for their hospital checkups? Can you clear an elderly couple's driveway during snow time? Can you clean their windows? Can you take them shopping, to the doctors, for an outing?

Trust your instincts. If you feel like something is wrong, don't be afraid to ask. Attend some training in your community on suicide, listening skills, drug and alcohol addiction, good parenting and so on. Be willing to listen without forcing advice. Sometimes one just needs to let it out.

Find resources in your community so you can help someone in need.

Remember to ensure your safety and that of those you love before getting involved in certain activities. Pray about it before you get involved. Make sure you hear from God clearly.

Give to charities, give to your local communities, hold tea parties in support of charities such as Cancer Research and Children in Need. If you are not in support of certain charities you can create and register one on behalf of the church.

Ways to reach out to others

(Please feel free to add to the list, this is just a guide).

- Start a youth, quiz, dance, music, drama group etc.
- An elderly people's coffee morning or lunch.
- Ministering to people who have been bereaved.
- Prison visitations.
- Hospital visitations.
- Being a buddy for lonely children.
- Fostering.
- Sponsoring a child or family.
- Host some art and craft fairs.
- Host some tea parties for a good cause.
- Going for outings.
- Holding some talent shows.
- Music festivals.
- Give the teenagers room to grow and to express themselves. Build them up spiritually with the word of God. Teach them to pray, empower them. Seek ways to sharpen their talent and encourage the shy ones.

Prayer Points

1. Lord, make me a friend.

2. Lord, open my heart and eyes to see the big picture.

3. Make me my brother and neighbour's keeper.

4. Give me time to do that which glorifies you.

5. Help me bring many to you because of the gifts you have blessed me with.

6. Remove any form of selfishness.

7. Help me enjoy the joy of serving you and your people.

What good is it
for someone
to gain the
whole world,
and yet lose
or forfeit
their very self?

Luke 9:25

Chapter 10
Dying to self

Overcoming offences is crucial if you want to grow within your church. Offences will come because you are working with human beings and you have to learn to forgive and move on. The others will need to accept your shortcomings and move on as well. Understanding that your church will never be faultless and that you too are not perfect will make your church a much better place to be.

There are so many silly and some genuine reasons why people get offended. I once had a friend who had been moving from one church to another complaining that the people were like this and that. He wanted to move to another church until I sat him down and lovingly explained to him that there is no such thing as a perfect church with perfect people or a perfect pastor. I told him about the personal things I had been through and how I had grown and benefited from them. I now know how to look out for people. I have learned the hard way but I will never forget to reach out. I told him that this could be a learning curve for him and maybe God was trying to sort something out in his life.

Reasons for leaving

People leave church for various reasons: maybe because they think the pastor does not like them, the pastor's wife is not nice, she overdresses or she dresses as if she is going gardening, the pastor and his wife drive beautiful expensive cars (it must be the church money!), or they did not feel welcome, they were ill and no one came to help or pray for them, they lost a loved one and there was no help given, the people overdress, the people do not smile enough, there are too many activities going on, there are too many children (noise levels are high), the church members are too old or too young, there are no single men or women, the music and prayer is too loud, they have too many single mothers, they pray quietly, they pray too much, the music is too dull, the leaders are always asking for money to buy things therefore they must love money too much. The list is endless.

One thing I know is that God wants us to walk in victory over offences. The devil celebrates and throws a party each time a believer leaves a church. Please, make sure you are not the one the offences come through:

> **"Woe to the world because of the things that cause people to stumble! Such things must come, but woe to the person through whom they come!"**
>
> **Matthew 18:7.**

Overcome offences

Offences will come but please remember that you are an overcomer. Do not let them pull you down. The word tells us that we are more than conquerors in Christ Jesus.

"Who shall separate us from the love of Christ? Shall trouble or hardship or persecution or famine or nakedness or danger or sword?
As it is written: 'For your sake we face death all day long; we are considered as sheep to be slaughtered.'

No, in all these things we are more than conquerors through him who loved us.
For I am convinced that neither death nor life, neither angels nor demons, neither the present nor the future, nor any powers, neither height nor depth, nor anything else in all creation, will be able to separate us from the love of God that is in Christ Jesus our Lord."

Romans 8:35-39.

Remember Christ has got good plans for us. Do not fall into the trap of the devil. Yes, I know it may be painful when people misunderstand you or judge you but remember they need help as much as you do.

How many times have you looked at someone and come to a wrong conclusion about them? We are human. We make mistakes but our problem is that we think the mistakes others make are much greater than ours.

We all need help. You are your brother's keeper. Take it as an opportunity to pray for them and bless their lives. If we all grasp that aspect of praying for each other, our lines will begin to fall in pleasant places for us and for those around us. We will also realise that we are not better than them. Our Bible clearly tells us to pray for those who persecute us.

> **"You have heard that it was said, 'Love your neighbour and hate your enemy.' But I tell you, love your enemies and pray for those who persecute you, that you may be children of your Father in heaven.**
> **He causes his sun to rise on the evil and the good, and sends rain on the righteous and the unrighteous.**
> **If you love those who love you, what reward will you get? Are not even the tax collectors doing that? And if you greet only your own people, what are you doing more than others?**
> **Do not even pagans do that?**
> **Be perfect, therefore, as your heavenly Father is perfect."**
>
> ## Matthew 5:43-48.

Once we learn to pray for them we begin to see clearly through the eyes of God because while we were yet sinners Christ loved us. Your attitude will change and they will be changed through your prayers.

> **"But God demonstrates his own love for us in this: While we were still sinners, Christ died for us."**
> **Romans 5:8.**

Sometimes God allows certain things to come our way in order to make us strong.

Do not hold on to grudges

Do not allow an offence to become a trap in your life. This can happen if you fail to forgive and move on or if you continue to focus on the wrongs that have been done by the person who has offended you. The devil enjoys bringing up past negative experiences and if he realises your weakest points (in fact he knows all your weaknesses and he feasts on them) he will make sure you will be offended by the slightest thing or remark that comes your way.

I understand that we can be hurt by others in the ministry or outside the ministry, but we should not focus on the wrongs. As a child of God you cannot afford to hold on to grudges.

How can you expect to be forgiven for your shortcomings when you do not forgive those who wrong you?

I personally think that anyone who refuses to forgive is mocking God. If God can forgive, who are you not to forgive?
Are you better than the Lord God Almighty?
Selah!

> **"Whenever you stand praying, forgive, if you have anything against anyone, so that your Father who is in heaven will also forgive you your transgressions."**
>
> **Mark 11:25.**

Whatever it is you are going through or have gone through the Lord is able to help, comfort and deliver you from self: but you have to be willing to allow Him to work in you and direct your path.

> **"The mind of man plans his way, But the LORD directs his steps."**
>
> **Proverbs 16:9.**

Let go and let God

Forgiveness is a choice and you have to make that decision. When we are facing challenges like an illness, loss of income, a separation, or a miscarriage, we always have faith that things will get better. We have faith and hope that God will heal us, we will get another job, we will get pregnant again and our marriage will work out fine. The same way we choose to forgive that fellow who has offended us is the same way we receive blessings from God. You need faith that the wound will heal.

Who told you that the church you are thinking of attending in future will be better than the one you are a member of right now? You don't know the people. It is like a marriage.
You will know their true colours when you move in with them.
You will never know if they snore until you share the same bed.
You will never know if they can cook until they cook something for you.
You will never know how angry they can get until you do something they do not like.
Because you love them you will hang in there.
You may buy some earplugs, invest in some cooking lessons or avoid the things you know your loved one does not like.
If a relationship with your spouse is worth fighting for, surely your relationship with God is also worth fighting for?
You cannot worship alone at home.

Whenever you go to his house you will always be richly blessed.

" Until I came into the sanctuary of God;
Then I perceived their end. Surely,
You set them in slippery places;
You cast them down to destruction.
How they are destroyed in a moment!
They are utterly swept away by sudden terrors!
Like a dream when one awakes,
O Lord, when aroused,
You will despise their form.
When my heart was embittered
And I was pierced within,
Then I was senseless and ignorant;
I was like a beast before You.

Nevertheless I am continually with You;
You have taken hold of my right hand.
With Your counsel You will guide me,
And afterward receive me to glory.
Whom have I in heaven but You?
And besides You, I desire nothing on earth. My
flesh and my heart may fail,
but God is the strength of my heart
and my portion forever.
For, behold, those who are far from
You will perish.

> **You have destroyed all those
> who are unfaithful to You.
> " But as for me, the nearness of God is my
> good; I have made the Lord GOD my refuge,
> That I may tell of all Your works."**
>
> **Psalm 73:17-28.**

Asaph was aware that envy was keeping him from seeing things the right way. He went into the sanctuary, the place of God's presence. It was there his understanding was increased and his short-sightedness healed. Note the key word in verse 17: 'until'. It was at the point when Asaph went into the sanctuary that he stopped thinking the way he had been thinking and began to look at things another way, God's way. He got a view of life on this earth through the Lord's eyes. God wants us to see things the way He does. He is love. He is forgiveness.

Seek God as Asaph did, asking for His guidance on every aspect of your life and not just offences.

I have noticed that a lot of people leave their jobs for various reasons. Those who are always in search of money will always be chasing a job that pays more. Those who leave because they did not get on with others will leave again for the same reasons. You need to deal with yourself and not shift blame onto others. What are you doing? What are you failing to do?
What could you do? Maybe you need to pray more!

I think the reason why some people get offended and end up leaving their church is because they do not understand God's purpose for putting them in that place. There is a reason why you are in that particular church. In a previous chapter I spoke about praying for God's guidance when choosing the church you should attend and also after joining the church to pray for direction as to which department you should serve in.

If you truly prayed before committing to a church and department, I think you should pray for God's guidance and His grace to stand fast and overcome. It is also great to have that good and faithful friend to strengthen and encourage you during trying times BUT I know a friend who sticks closer than a brother and His name is Jesus Christ. You can lean on Him when you are not strong. He will carry you through it all and you will conquer.

Pray for guidance

If you clearly heard from God about joining this church then it means you are going to miss out on the blessings God has in store for you in that ministry. If you are not sold out to anything or someone then you can easily pack your bags and go. If you are sold out then you will be willing to stand, pray and to fight the good fight. I like to look at a ministry the same way I look at a marriage. You are praying for a permanent place of worship, you know what you are after, you see a place you like or hear about it from someone, you attend, you like it, and you become a committed member. In a marriage, you will be praying for a marriage partner, you know what you are looking for, you meet someone, you like them, you get to know them, you are sure he or she is the one because God has confirmed it, you get married. Two years down the line something you do not like happens in church or someone offends you, so you decide to leave. But when you prayed, God said yes, this was the place. Now because you have been offended you decide to leave. Has God changed? What is God saying about the situation? Why must you leave if this is the place where God wants you to be?

If you have a misunderstanding with your better half do you pack your bags and go? Most of us will stay and work it out. We'll go for counselling and move on together.

Why must you leave the place God has guided you to because of offences? Offences come, offences go, but it is how you deal with them that determines how far you will go in life and with God. Just because you have argued with someone or you made a suggestion that was not accepted does not mean you are not appreciated. You need to die to self. It is not about you but Christ. You are there to serve.

This is the reason why I strongly encourage you to listen to God before making a move. The devil will always try to offend you, he knows all your weaknesses and he will try to use them to manipulate you.

You are bigger than that. You are a conqueror in Christ. Greater is He that is in you, than he that is in this world. If God has not spoken to you concerning the place where He has sent you, stay put and serve joyfully and gracefully. I am not saying it will be easy but I know it will be worth it and you will grow spiritually.

> **"You are from God, little children, and have overcome them; because greater is He who is in you than he who is in the world." 1 John 4:4.**

Live to love, live to forgive

Stay focused on the big picture—the big picture is JESUS CHRIST. Live to love. Live to forgive and seek to bring souls into the Kingdom of God. Never let church politics weigh you down through offences or whatever else that goes on, but keep your focus on Jesus.

The church is the place where you and your family are ministered the most. The devil will try all he can to keep you and your loved ones from God's presence. This is the reason why he will always try to offend you, especially at church. In fact look at offences as a trap from the devil. His aim is to distract you from doing and enjoying what God wants you to do. God has called you to be in your church for a reason: you are not there for a season.

It is God who orders your steps and not the devil. God wants us to forgive anyone who offends us. You have to choose to forgive, let go and move on.

> **"And whenever you stand praying,**
> **if you have anything against anyone forgive**
> **him, that your Father in heaven**
> **may also forgive you your trespasses."**
> **Mark 11:25.**

I like this quote from Mother Teresa:

"People are often unreasonable and self-centred.

Forgive them anyway.

If you are kind, people may accuse you of ulterior motives.

Be kind anyway.

If you are honest, people may cheat you.

Be honest anyway.

If you find happiness, people may be jealous.

Be happy anyway.

The good you do today may be forgotten tomorrow.

Do good anyway.

Give the world the best you have and it may never be enough. Give your best anyway. For you see, in the end, it is between you and God. It was never between you and them anyway."

Prayer Points

1. Give me the grace not to bear grudges.
2. Give me the grace and heart to forgive.
3. Ask for God to be your guide and vision.
4. Show me the big picture like you did to Asaph.
5. Help me to love more and to focus on you alone.
6. Teach me perseverance.
7. Remove every selfish bone in me.
8. Even when offended give me the grace to overcome the offences and to continue to serve you with a smile.
9. May I never undermine my pastor's leadership and all the decisions he makes.

Chapter 11
Building healthy relationships

For any group of people to be able to walk and work together, there needs to be a relationship. It could be a working relationship based on company ethics, or a relationship based on friendship or marriage. There need to be some guidelines on how to keep that relationship going. Bringing out the best in any relationship, where you create awesome rapport with the other person or group of people is determined by how much you put in or are willing to give in order to connect.

Christianity is defined by lifestyles and relationships that follow the teachings of Jesus Christ. These teachings are based on the love that was found and seen in His teachings and His life. For example, His dying for us. Him coming down to stay on earth and live a life just like you and me.

For you to be able to have a good and healthy relationship with your pastor and other members of the church I strongly encourage you to try as much as you can to build a sound relationship with all the people you come in contact with.

This should not be because you may want something from them in the future but just because the Word of God tells us:

> "...how wonderful and pleasant it is when brothers live together in harmony."
> **Psalm 133:1.**

And:

> "I appeal to you, brothers,
> in the name of our Lord Jesus Christ,
> that all of you agree with one another
> so that there may be no divisions among you
> and that you may be perfectly united
> in mind and in thought."
>
> **1 Corinthians 1:10.**

Learn from your relationships

Good communication is the life-blood of every relationship. Disagreements are natural and normal. A healthy relationship is an evolving relationship in which each partner is in a position to learn and grow, and often we learn and grow best through the conflicts. If both partners are willing to learn, conflict can provide fertile ground for learning and growing rather than a way to control or avoid being controlled by the other.

When you learn to love, care and connect with yourself and God you're already doing the best you can to make yourself happy. When you are happy you will also desire to make peace with everyone else so you can continue to leave a peaceful and joyful life.

Forgiveness is essential to building healthy relationships as it frees one's mind from unnecessary heartache and stress. Failure to forgive results in people going their separate ways. Without forgiveness one cannot be free with the other because there will always be a skeleton in the cupboard waiting to resurface at the least of provocations. Two cannot walk together unless they agree. Honesty is another very basic element to a healthy relationship. The consequences of what has happened do not matter. We all make mistakes because we are human, but taking responsibility for our actions and being prepared to face the consequences is a sign of maturity.

Pride or a superiority complex can hinder good relationships. If you wrong someone, apologise. It does not matter whether it is your child, a junior at work, your employee, a student or a friend, just apologise! It proves that you are human and that you make mistakes. You will earn more respect from them. Pride can cost you good relationships or friendships. Be willing to be corrected and be approachable.

I am not asking you to put yourself in a vulnerable position, but you should be humble enough to accept correction and to apologise.

Prayer Points

1. Lord, make me a relationship builder.

2. May I be honest and trustworthy in all my dealings.

3. Help me to be a peacemaker wherever I go.

4. Help me to respect others.

5. May I give my all in everything I do.

6. Help me to be the best teammate ever.

7. Whether my pastor or teammates are present or not may I always strive for excellence in all my doings.

8. May I be a good example of a disciple.

9. Give me wisdom to work joyfully and peacefully with all.

10. May I never undermine my pastor's decisions and leadership.

Chapter 12
Prophesy positively over your church

Each time I hear my children discuss the power of words among themselves my soul rejoices. We are always careful with the things we say to one another, family and friends. I often tell my children that if anyone says anything they do not agree with they should reject it in Jesus' name. I always encourage them to never nurse any negativity at all.

> "The Lord GOD has given Me
> The tongue of the learned,
> That I should know how to speak
> A word in season to him who is weary.
> He awakens Me morning by morning,
> He awakens My ear
> To hear as the learned."
>
> Isaiah 50:4.

Watch your words

Words are the vehicles through which we communicate our thoughts one to another. The tongue is just the driver and because of that it drives us to our destiny. Moving in spiritual maturity requires us to learn and master the use of the right words for the right reason and in the right season.

If you'd really like to master the art of a positive tongue, you must seek guidance from the Holy Spirit. Try prayer and fasting. It is not easy to tame one's tongue unless you ask for help from the Spirit of God.

"8 But no man can tame the tongue. It is an unruly evil, full of deadly poison.

"9 With it we bless our God and Father, and with it we curse men, who have been made in the similitude of God.

"10 Out of the same mouth proceed blessing and cursing. My brethren, these things ought not to be so.

"11 Does a spring send forth fresh water and bitter from the same opening?

"12 Can a fig tree, my brethren, bear olives, or a grapevine bear figs? Thus no spring yields both salt water and fresh."

James 3:8-12.

From the verses above we can see that it is not easy to tame our tongue but it is possible with God's help. If we belong to God we must be well-disciplined.

We are told in 1 Peter 1:15-18:

"15 But now you must be holy in everything you do, just as God who chose you is holy. 16 For the Scriptures say, 'You must be holy because I am holy.'

"17 And remember that the heavenly Father to whom you pray has no favourites. He will judge or reward you according to what you do. So you must live in reverent fear of him during your time as 'foreigners in the land.' 18 For you know that God paid a ransom to save you from the empty life you inherited from your ancestors. And the ransom he paid was not mere gold or silver."

If you really desire to be a blessing to your church or to be used by God mightily you must learn to speak God's word over your pastor and the church every day. The same way you pray faithfully over your children, spouse, and business.

Look for positive Bible verses:

"With the fruit of a man's mouth his stomach will be satisfied; He will be satisfied with the product of his lips. Death and life are in the power of the tongue, and those who love it will eat its fruit." Proverbs 18:21.

Do you want to enjoy being a member of your church?
Then always remember that we eat our words and they become our life's harvest. What we allow to come out of our mouths greatly determines what we 'eat' in life. Words are like seeds that go before you, planting your future for life or for death.

If you speak the word of God, unity, love, peace, joy, abundance, and faith, spiritual gifts will appear. The power to make something good of the church lies within you.
What you say will have either a positive or negative impact. The more you speak positively the more sweet things you reap and the sweeter your life will become.

In Psalms 122:1, King David said:

"I was glad when they said to me, 'Let us go to the house of the LORD'."

I would like to believe it was because of his positive attitude towards the things of God. He was serving God faithfully. Though he had his own problems he did not allow them to stop him praising the Lord. You should delight in serving your God and be able to speak positively to others and His church.

Prophesy daily over your church

- Prophesy daily that your church is touching your city, your country and the entire world.
- Prophesy that all your church's needs are met in abundance with plenty of overflow to bless others too.
- Prophesy over your pastor that God will continue to grant her wisdom and to continue to be a blessing to His church. (God's church).
- Prophesy for open doors and soul winning. Ask for guidance on how to reach out to different types of people.
- Prophesy that your church will become a mighty power in your community. (People in authority will come to it to seek for guidance, advice and prayer from the church before making any decision concerning your city or country).
- Prophesy that people will hear of the good work that is happening in your church.
- Prophesy the restoration of marriages.
- Prophesy the so-called barren getting pregnant.
- Prophesy the sick getting healed.
- Prophesy that addicts are liberated from their addictions.

"The hand of the LORD was upon me, and He brought me out by the Spirit of the LORD and set me down in the middle of the valley; and it was full of bones. 2 He caused me to pass among them round about, and behold, there were very many on the surface of the valley; and lo, they were very dry. 3 He said to me, 'Son of man, can these bones live?'

And I answered, 'O Lord GOD, You know.' 4 Again He said to me, 'Prophesy over these bones and say to them, 'O dry bones, hear the word of the LORD.' 5 Thus says the Lord GOD to these bones, 'Behold, I will cause breath to enter you that you may come to life. 6 I will put sinews on you, make flesh grow back on you, cover you with skin and put breath in you that you may come alive; and you will know that I am the LORD.'

"7 So I prophesied as I was commanded; and as I prophesied, there was a noise, and behold, a rattling; and the bones came together, bone to its bone. 8 And I looked, and behold, sinews were on them, and flesh grew and skin covered them; but there was no breath in them. 9 Then He said to me, 'Prophesy to the breath, prophesy, son of man, and say to the breath,
'Thus says the Lord GOD, "Come from the four winds, O breath, and breathe on these slain, that they come to life."'
10 So I prophesied as He commanded me, and the breath came into them, and they came to life and stood on their feet, an exceedingly great army."

Ezekiel 37:1-10.

I love to speak positively over my children and the church and see things begin to fall into pleasant places. It gives me great joy when I hear my pastor or leader preach exactly the same message. You can make a difference too. Just ask God to transform your tongue into a wellspring of life. Ask God to help you, so that no unhealthy talk comes out of your mouth but only that which is helpful for building up others and yourself.

> **"Don't use foul or abusive language. Let everything you say be good and helpful, so that your words will be an encouragement to those who hear them."**
>
> **Ephesians 4:29.**

"Servants, be submissive
to your masters
with all fear,
not only to the good and gentle,
but also to the harsh."

1 Peter 2:18.

Chapter 13
Pastor's Appreciation

Since I have started maturing in the things of the Lord I have come to understand and appreciate what my pastor does for me. My pastor is always there for me. I can always text and call him. The time he has invested in praying for me and my family is amazing and I know he prays for others too.

We need to appreciate our pastors and show them that we are grateful to have them in our church and lives. Pastors never get paid what they deserve. They do so many jobs and yet they do not get paid that much. Dealing with human beings from various cultural backgrounds with different temperaments is not an easy job. Show your appreciation for your pastor. If your church is blessed with several pastors, remember them also. Buy them a card or flowers to show your support and encouragement. It is good to celebrate your pastor's birthday, anniversary, as well as Mother's and Father's days.

"Let each of you look out not only for his own interests, but also for the interests of others."

Philippians 2:4.

Celebrate your pastor

Sometimes people can be so self-centred. All they want is to get something from their pastor or leader. They never give back. They are like a waste bin that is only there to receive and never to give. Now is the time to reflect and think of all the things your pastor has done for you in the past few months and years and begin to thank God for that pastor, for his life, his family, his job, his ministry and all that concern him.

My church has a pastor's appreciation week. I remember one year when I went to my local Christian bookstore to buy something for my pastor. I got engaged in a discussion with one of the shop assistants and he was amazed by the fact that our church had an appreciation week. I did not know what to say about the purpose of pastor's appreciation week. I had never thought about it. I had just felt it was the right thing to do.

As I left the shop I started thinking about the appreciation week and about how different people might look at it.

It is truly good to celebrate your pastor. I strongly encourage members whose church has a Pastor's Appreciation Day, Week or Month to celebrate it wholeheartedly. Apart from telling your pastor that you love, appreciate or thank her, why don't you do something much more than just give her a card or a Bible verse figurine?

I had bought my pastor a bible verse figurine/plaque but never thought of praying to find out what I should do for him or buy for him. I never thought of inquiring from the Lord to get a revelation of what my pastor's needs were at that time. I realised that I had been selfish in my giving. I just blindly went ahead and bought something that seemed appropriate until a stranger challenged me.

Create a special service for her. Take him out for dinner.

Appreciate your pastor by making your own discipleship journey a priority. Attend a small group or Bible study gathering with an open mind to learn and to inspire. Consider saying, "Yes!" when one of the pastors approach you about starting a new ministry. Find something within the church that you enjoy doing and build on it.

Your pastor needs encouragement all the time. A church will not do well unless it has dedicated members.

Unless church members prepare their hearts to worship and to be transformed by God, the church cannot thrive or move forward. A church will not grow financially unless it has one of the best finance teams in the world. Are you the person to head that department? Are you the evangelist? Are you ready, available and willing?

A church will not thrive until someone is willing to teach the children's Sunday school, or if there is no one willing to meet and greet or show visitors where to sit when they come in for church service.

A church cannot thrive if its members do not share the same vision with their pastor or leader.

A church is only as strong as its disciples. Below are just a few signs of good discipleship:

- People who give regularly even if there are a million things they could do with their money because they know that God is their provider and that all they have came from Him.
- People who show up even when weekend plans could easily take them away, because they believe they are there to make a difference.
- People who serve even when they think their gifts are not required or important enough to offer, because they trust God to multiply their offerings.

These are just a few of the actions that will truly help your pastor continue to serve with joy for years to come and they mean much more than the gifts you can give him during any Pastor's Appreciation Week!

My Prayer for my Pastor during Appreciation Week

O Lord my God,

I thank you for my Pastor.

I also pray for all those whom you have appointed to be leaders over your church.

Bless him with wisdom, love, grace, strength and the zeal to lead by example and to accomplish Your will.

May he always remember to give You praise and to worship You wholeheartedly.

May his will be knitted in Your will.

May he continually seek you and take time out of his busy schedule to hear Your voice.

May You increase his faith daily.

May You renew his strength and the love he bestows on others by pouring out Your love in his heart and life.

May he always be glad that You called him.

May he continue to dwell under Your shelter, O Lord thou Most High.

May humility and holiness always be his portion.

Guide and protect him from all forms of evil all the days of his life.

Strengthen his faith day by day.

May humility and the fear of God always be his portion.

May he always seek Your help in any area of his life; concerning his family, our church, serving the community, our nation and all over the world.

Watch over his family, encourage him and may he always walk in You as You are the Light.

May Your word always be the lamp that guides his feet.

Thank you Lord for my pastor.

In Jesus' Mighty Name I pray.

Amen.

Prayer Points

1. Lord, help me to be trustworthy. (Please make me someone my pastor or leader can trust).
2. Lord, if you can use anything you can use me. (I am available to be used by you).
3. Lord, help me to serve you in spirit and in truth.
4. Lord, guide me in all the decisions I make.
5. Lord, help me to see people the way you do and to always seek for the good in them.
6. Lord, reign in me.
7. Lord, help me to always be positive.
8. Lord, give me love so I can show mercy and be compassionate just like You.
9. Lord, grant me the desire to win souls.
10. Lord make me an amiable destiny helper.
11. Lord purify me.
12. Lord cleanse me.
13. Lord overshadow me.
14. Lord mend me.
15. Heal my heart Oh God!
16. Make me whole and sin free.

About the author

Roselie Emmanuel is an Assistant Pastor in RCCG's Fountain of Love Parish, Fraserburgh, Scotland. She lives in Aberdeen with her husband Pastor Wilfred and their two sons Shane and Seth. This is her first book.

www.ingramcontent.com/pod-product-compliance
Lightning Source LLC
Chambersburg PA
CBHW070952080526
44587CB00015B/2270